Planted and Formed

Jay Nunnery

Cyberwit.net
HIG 45 Kaushambi Kunj, Kalindipuram
Allahabad - 211011 (U.P.) India
http://www.cyberwit.net
Tel: +(91) 9415091004
E-mail: info@cyberwit.net

Printed at Vcore.

Contents

Forgiveness

trust yourself
as music in
the world's
forever
pending geometry
seesawing on metallic light
driven insane
its heat rising
like a tiger
in the jungle
having caught
a whiff
of some long-sought
prey
its mouth
watering small drops
that ruffle
its fur
on perfected instinct
vibrantly as the sequencing
all the chromosomes
thread into time
stamping them with
God's signature
holy like the saved

Hawaiian Vibes

Diamondstars cycle
To the tune of fullness

Lost in the waves like
Ships created with tweezers

In a glass bottle by believers
In order to help

As the sky's foundation
Lays homeward and like

An old song
or was it a billboard

I loved gratefully
It doesn't matter

Boats in the middle of an ocean's
Glimmering noon

As long as we are safe
The love songs say so

We need nothing
Singing to the roll up

Everyone knows who they are
Changing colors with their eyes

Deep impressionistic thankfulness
By some extension everything

Is everything

I am free

You are freedom

My body contains what is mine
And what is not

I love you and I am sorry
Forgive me and thank you

The Same

Bobbing to the bumps,
Struggling uphill, with

Those days, back within
Salvation, the Clearing
Becoming more visible,
As our rider's altered love

Deep down,
The Clearing realizing
The only way's unlimited
Distance, fingers stretched,

From hand and arms stretched
Life-like, bobbing to
The bumps
Struggling uphill, becoming

More visible and destined
For all those restated beliefs
And old prayers, burnished
Replacements to the mosaic.

The backyard sloped
And then sloped once more.
A pair of white porches saw all
Of the soaring and anointings—

A mirage's congregation.
As the words changed
The meanings changed.
It's best not to remember?

Or the bloodless eternal
Respites persuade us to
Journey, tracing the loop
With our flesh, threading

Mind and Body and Soul.
In a way,
I mean breathe deeply.
My father told me.

You

The beauty returns—hope put back into acceptance.
Every dream we've shared grows strength in being ours.
Dreams the size of oceans reflect light. We are stars.
We are what gets looked at and deemed too far away
and we are made of the same thing, some periodic,
oddly named, and elemental chemicals. They won't know,
as I am all the way gone. Dance on the stage.
If you fall, we will catch you.
Fractured and fragmented, the show must go on
because it will come together. Have the views.
Think millions. Think big and be in love with your
thoughts as creative as the birds gliding
through their flight. Change. Be brave as the solider.
You are wrapped in armor, always been hallowed.
Keep the secrets. Saying nothing is called silence
and silence—they say—is golden. Think gold.
Think gratefully. Gratitude approaches all
understanding and leads to that place that is
called Heaven. When you and that narration happen,
you can be in control. Believe the truth.
You establish your truth, untouchable and in the spirit,
as a casted beacon somewhere so far ahead you must run to it.

Destiny Conducting Forever

expanding a willow's
salvation and the distance

from hope to love
the night tightroping

along a line drawn in the sand
knowing that it is unlikely that we'll

resist pressing our ears
to the angel's outpouring

their righteousness unbounding
a promised justice

interacting with galaxy-clusters
and their guarded judgment

and their nomadic and ascending
equity converting like Sunday mornings

widening and narrowing
each time with more anticipation

this rounded affinity celebrated in
lives led as symmetrical enterprises

fused with the shared and unshared
compensations for the hourglasses' delays

Living

I'd picked a rose
and a rose grew
in front of me
its red petals the size
of elephant ears

It had no thorns

And the fallen and
standing surrounded us

beckoning more
sunlight—my rose

had been before
drained from then
to now—optimistically
eclipsed as a golden

moon spinning from another
universe's sun—mine—

would keep on being
forever—stalked out

replacing the torch
guiding the saints

to the sufferers
crying wax to get lost

in the earth as the
celebration lived

Upright

Clock's hands digitize favor
Patterns alter on the ground

An ex making each segment equal
—Count the stars

Orion's blood dripping
Above into the night

The chill's countenance
Puncturing my conscious

Carrying on with orders

Paint brushes are wands
Sweeping and beautiful things

Perfecting love
Choosing to ride
Instead of walk
Young love

In a dark that's past midnight
It is theirs
The sensational repenting
Light shining through lips

Time As Nothing Worth Holding Onto

Knowing that you serve as the new standard is innovation.

There are no walls.
There are no ceilings—

As the cushiony purple

Goes to the starlight, which comes in
Through windows like music

And all you can do is it.

Once I Thought

I knew less than I did
Now I know faith
As the receiving
The burn on my arm
That was so long ago
Sunlight approaching
Through mountains
Of souls that move

Kiss

To fly as angels
Full of displaced

Dreaming about the future
Waiting for you in the sky

Overheard and unspoken
A so-called secret
A beginning undone
Seen within signs

As if to be was
The only answer left

Sumatra

Staying to sing, the forgotten, the buried mended,
the idea appeared, gentle, as a part of another idea.

A flag in that silence
A song wanting to be

Repeated as the soul
Of nothingness or everything

Whenever everything matters
The blending in more
Like being
The sky both night and day

New Mercies

Reasons afire
Easier than origami

Since we
Are together

In this
I bid you

Ever-expanding
The table presented

Time After Morning

Luminosity within
    on an angel holding cell's wall

Balancing

Hatred   &
                        Art

Humor
                                &
Pain

An old man with more hair than me and a fidget
that's overtaken him after so many things calling whoever was
left
clothed in the same blues as me beams

Silence followed
    on my strength's incensement

By reason
I did it
naked and in spite of limits
refusing to eat
having fasted towards
seeing the all that is
as though this is
"all that"

Of all
I didn't expect watercolors
on the ride home

I should have

no longer
the mystery finished
like a patchwork's emblem

Local Sources

my mirror shows the hollowness of eternity
specks of stardust trailing into the sunrise

a regained smile bubbling like champagne
needing something clear to contain it

forced through the air
as abandoned dreams
upon the awakened
old idea that's nobody's

begging like those prayers
a soul singer might sing
about a supplication to be
expressed like the wind

expresses itself in the trees
sometimes saying you will
and you have and
you are

Voiceless Ghosts Floated Through Our Heads

A shared memory cherished itself for survival
Time moved as directionless as the wind
Every realm had existences of highs and lows
It will all hold us we decided once on the river
Breeze drifted through and spread the lavenders
Rain and dispersing went on with the waves
We went on in a song about the spirits' waves

Three Stars

Angels' wings
Flap me cool

Soulful things on
Soulful tools

Cain and
Abel

Baby born
Dominating label

I internalize them
When I'm awake

Michael's warm
And righteous sake

Word revelations
Minutely dispatched

Stand for those
Truly attached

Being Comforted

The last step is always
the easiest to take.
Due to your momentum,
the logic which proceeded
uncoils and you know where
you are. The door's weight
doesn't matter and the world
fades away. Breakable and dark,
entering upon the room
you've been inside before,
you become aware of the depth
and the openness expands
like numbers. You want
to count upward, to get higher
as you go. The seat rests
there but you don't notice it
until you turn a few times in place.
The look her brown eyes
gives you feelings
like creative inspiration
but you become
aware that
those eyes
were just a memory
and you decide to sit and let
more memories wash from your head.
The memories fall to your feet and rise
to become a drowning in their clarity.
One, two, three, four, five is how it goes.
Then you need another hand.
More help comes and you know.

They Will Love You

Patience kept
In the quiet
Corner waits
For the dreamer

Which they carry
As love and reason
Will hold
Onto them

As though the truth
Were reason enough

Skin correlating
With life
Opening eyes
Seeing art

Within art
Not understanding

The miracle
That beginnings

Possess
Minds

Grown into the infinite
Patterning hypotheticals
Contradicting reality
Depleted in ways of being

Basketball

The points
Aim to center,

Guarding circles
Possessions hanging

As though in mid-fall,
Playing to be made.

Suggesting wholeness,
Achieved in an instant,

Fireworks shot magically
Like one stone hitting two

Birds at different stages
Of their legend in a world

That ends so suddenly
And phases. However,

Man endures, the glory
Belonging in the—eternally nestled,

Curling with inhales and exhales—
Beyond, a past that was never seen.

Drive hard.
Don't travel.

Icy White

Trust challenges
Solidifying into glass

Which raises without
Reason only to fall lower
Than ever within
And higher without

Reason—at some points

Nothing more than
Wings in a dreary sky

The flock spinning like vinyl

Captured in an after party
Of imagined fragments

Building blocks flashing
Strobing lights to intoxicate
The dance's ritualistically letting go
The Reborn—reversing to slow

Backwards into The Ethereal

Ebbing as unrecognized and melting
Currents in the troublesome
Night's storms, as I saw—
As clear as I've seen anything—

And You Know Why Love Awakens Those Shores

The embers render tonight's
Unrequited love
Spent on a bag of almonds

The stars gazing down as telling
Constellations speak for the moment
Enough grace is driving now

Like a spaceship and light in sky
Then nothing was to be done
As faith trailing and leading

Hope without cause like a prince's
Crown fitting only
The future which is now

Simple desire fulfilled to the same
Set of notes that creates those songs
As the wind does those waves

The Latter House's Glory

Eschewed as something misspelled and lied into correction,
the gambler, the addict, flooded by the warming, dies,

doing what he loved, without his family. I am someone
else because I knew before and I am alive.

Therefore, my heart broke open like a receiver
whose defender has fallen down field. Remember

the painting of the black woman with peace signs in her eyes
and flowers in her hair? Children

went unschooled, learning what summer felt like
through harvest, laughing as if their punchlines

needed no setups. Returned to the appointed time,
at the old spot, avoiding varmints, iotas teaching

small lakes about vastness, running over snow-water,
hearing about it again and again, having heard about it

again and again, I know that this is peace, changes
like political doctrines as doubt stretches towards

wisdom's abundance, regimented as rolling stones
surrounded by clean lakes before me, answered

as a windfall, the maelstrom, and their provocation
and North Carolina's capital and an empty prognosis.

Anonymous

Meditating at night,
I find peace in an actor's response,

supporting the exiles,
vexing the taken pieces

of time like a surprising move.
Consecrations, above the soul too,

pollinating and germinating and flowering,
humanely commune with my awe.

Considering meditation,
I find glory in now's questions,

an appeal in names that belong to all,
reproaching iniquity like a palette of deliverances,

swelling and departing
weeps of consumed discrimination

as though the stars' and the moon's
wholeheartedness praised the sleeping birds—

beaks tucked and feathers beneath
feathers and dreaming of melodies

and the fish that rest, good dreams
that befall within each other,

dwelling as messages do in angels
and as angels in neighborhoods.

Once Upon A Time In Music

shadows bouncing
in the fray
onto torn metal's
spotty mahogany

cascade as the night
identifies its operatic

Truth

where the lovers grow old
fielding togetherness

walking by the school's
emergency holding hands

Cellular

Light deemed
me Holy, lost
blues, clamoring
to Speak but Words
wave white flags

I should have told Myself more

I run my hands over the holes
I'd punched into the wall

Sadness is a broken heart
blood racing uninstructed
Selves fragmented in Light
dreamy day upon night

I began comprehending movements
as fugues, as masculine and feminine,
as those one might find in dreams,
and I could not interpret a thing.

The weather changed every day.
When you're right they won't
let you be a politician.

The Cuts Taped Together

And unless it expands,
Warps outwardly—

Unless it blooms
As though from a seed

With undying roots
In love with the soil,

Eased sense of when
To become and when

To get
Over

Thank You

A model
Actress
Who cannot
Handle the stress

Without a handle
A passion to dismantle

And express
A preference
To make you
Guess

When she is at
Your residence

With questions
That have
No answers
Something about

Some dancers
Of the exotic

Variety
In this
Biotic
Society

Rejoice

past dusk into a streetlight's reforming supremacy
when the bodies don't do and the love we hold,
inhaled from the leaves
like warmth, go up as haloes

over
our cold ears
somewhere
                  between,
a routine

subscribed its own royalty,
manifesting in Goliaths and camels and tigers

By The Nile's opulent flowing.
Gold cries forward

Carrying circuits to the designs hovering,
Wolflike flesh—forgive—

from a place where no one knows
so quickly and freely that we don't even make it around—
somewhere
Jackie Robinson steals home
Brooklyn like Los Angeles when the whole wide world
is spreading

L   o   v   e,

at the same time
like a movement

choreographed to a thrown stone's rippling
as it plops into The Nile

like it would
The Mississippi

Seeking, Believing, Still

Appear unto me
Crashing public displays
Of born wilderness
Where the poor solicit money
And mourners melt provoked
Spheres of time and inheritances
That speak not by heavens
Enthroned in guts of white owls
Looking to the night anew
Above the world as my feet dangle

Behold

Departing from St. Mary's—
plead the snow's conceived as wool—

so many instruments played,
were upheld, under oaks that shielded
us and covered the black Jaguar

as though fate's shadow,
bound to encircle,
revolts of unfaithfulness
attempting to save themselves—

one last time perhaps.
I will never really know
like pledges given
to no one here, torn

from eternity instead,
revived in stories told
differently each time,
the rooftops considering

our hearts, testifying to pride
and snakeskins. A journey
for the sake of the road and one
for the sake of wanting to get lost.

Separated like the humble,
chastised on the pavement,

we made everything, delivered
what I found in multiplied visions,

turning, fading.
Forgotten trips,
vacations on
trains, exalted
by golden wings,
and a hat of
early acceptance—
take it all away

and receive me graciously,
stolen because we don't know,

transforming like a child learning
alone and out of necessity.

When the withering began,
I was acting with my eyes.

I punched the prized bear
until its stuff floated down

to the unfinished concrete.
Again, this time because

of the music
my own gift

plucked and latched
around my neck

and it was stolen too
as though the saint
could not before
but he could now—

for gold
just like the outlaw.

Ironically, the director
couldn't bear a good lie.
Just as I cannot untangle
its borders resting on

more and more land

all the way to Monona.

But mourning shakes out
gratefulness. The days come.

Bean

If your wisdom stretches without,
You are a teacher,

Gentle branched and always considering summer.
If your wisdom stretches within,

You are an influence,
Leading shine and the walker's next step.

If you conquer the field,
You have moved through love,

Persuaded by eternity and its contemplation
Holding agony like I've held a pomegranate seed.

If you conquer yourself,
You are strong,

Found just before the preposition's arrival
And in an indivisible togetherness—

Happiness as wealth, robust as the future,
Originated in the real's projecting.

Daze Won Amongst Salvation's Newfound Carelessness

In letting go there is power
Like a flower
Next to another flower

As the leaves change colors and fall
The streets as empty as the mall

Arcade lights flicker in my mind
Prompted on disaster brought from the divine
Somewhere between each line
As the saying goes
Flows
The interconnected transfixed coloration
Of velvet red to royal violet buried in creation
Too good to be true
Moments too pure not to be you

Meaningfully addressed to nowhere
A translation lost to vocations and prayer

Raised Exchanges

Friends forming, getting guiltlessness, they say things,
waving their $5-10 shades through the murmuring air,
pointing out the window. Precious jazz plinks over other
choice words. Embellished and Beatlesque, living

love lives, abandoned, their minds, ordain the wayward.
Obtaining the multiplication of vague redirections
to the gut and the breath, grinding an awakening
fragrance through ongoing ventilation, endeavors

noted in the margins of a first edition, concocted over
homemade old fashioneds, sweet, too many, all theirs.

Capitalize

Dreamland in my
kindred coldness

sacred transformed
to the beat of a different song,

introduced with drums and voice,
a submariner's times, the oceanic blues

of a soul set on fire
a promise pillared

in love
appearing

as a lion's doctrine.
A woman

whose name I know,
posing on the roof,

looks like she found the gumption
to jump, her gold lustered

in the turbulence's rumbling
rawness, splattering half-truth.

Her gold would flood the streets too.
The summer purifies.

If she doesn't jump, I say
we shoot her down—

with bows and arrows
and for irony's sake.

Realism

Known by many,
seen as unframed
and unsold, nevertheless,
a theater is above evenly,

as unframed and unsold.
In a little while, I will not

see either of them again,
but if I wait and continue

walking through the day's
dampness, right before
the darkness, filled with
fairs and drunkenness

and—today especially—
the let loose, I will

see both again, though
in a different order.

The Universes Between Themes

The time
It takes
A heartbroken
Seashell that I
Want to press
My ear to if
Only to impress
My kingdom
Like Lear
For you

Fair Trade Around Noon

Signified by these vehicles
            that seem
      to be
getting closer
      no matter which way they are going
outwardly patience,
correlating the clouds
                  and telling stories that light the sky

about existential stoicism and rational Taoism and relative Buddhism
and angst's manifesto and logic's intrinsic lightness, given surpris-
ingly from young to old
                              turns in the midst
                              of a snowfall like a ballerina
on a philharmonic and bare stage
head lifted to the colossal,
      beams and wires and spotlights and platforms,
peeling paint
warm and cold
metal. It waited
for the gold key around its love-giver's neck to turn to jasper.
            Written along her spine are proclamations, thousands
and thousands—
            Grape-fueled cessation drifting into a woven night
                  securing conciliation in their floating.
I tower
until noon,

revering tears
dried in tomorrow's
former planet.

Opening Sounds

My hands lay like a sleepy construction worker
on the toasty side of the bed,

taken away from thought,
blessing brought by going,

acclimating an unmanned speech,
plucking instruments coming together

as the clouds are already. One song
divides into something that can be

spread over, encrusted
in more skipped lines

full of good and bad fortune.
The same smile crosses every face.

The sky is a body, exhaling dilemma,
an acknowledgment lost between too many

as *it is not said*

but written that I already do,
a matching magenta sharing

offense as my hands
get up and let go

of everything.
Perhaps, if I didn't know

that I should not care,
I would. Holding only

this (now that) pen for now
(now then), I accept the test,

understanding that—as all
things must—I too must pass.

Each Hand's Hole

The sun chills
Shining through the cold
If you're too young to get old

It's not personal
When my thoughts turn to you
Because now I know what to do

Returning

From staring at the sun
To falling into tide

Still not knowing what
I did not know

Victory bitter on my tongue
The indigos bless me in ways
Incapacitated in timelessness
My whole heart propelling
Praise into each chamber
Speeding into the past
When you were there
I am but I should proclaim
My faith in parts of my spirit that still shine
Wondering what is going to happen
Save the children if nothing else

Everlastingness

Only light can do
Introspecting
Turns downhill for a new thing, already underfoot,

Mourning the loss of the sufferer
Dying for the 999th time

Tonight is like a line
Practicing healing astigmatisms
The Garner Park shelter a shared kingdom
A place for good that I run to with both hands up

Too fast
With laughter

As above so below

I am dancing like Fred Astaire between brooms with Prince's
voice in my ears
For those in the hurricane
     For those who are suffering oppression
          For those who are experiencing death

Energy answers with harbingering
A felt compassion that expands like a forever-true thought
A believed prayer
Something to soften the heart that has been wounded by the
dealer's greed

Time and judgment
There's nothing like them

Namesake

The night slinks its aspiration and restless hopes of dreaming
About morning deftly into time

I hope for you
That usually stays starless

Those generations wheel
    The imminent entailing
            Blues as spiritual

Run
Look
Believing
In turns
As systems revel

I want you

I have since you told me that you did run and look and believe

    I remember when you told me even
My memory was retractable

You told me about a small frame over a tree too
And you told me that the clouds smell like myrrh too

Everything Is Everything

Shadows mantle the cheap table
Orange and wildflowers dip over
A glass pumpkin reflects dim light

Words pile on the counter
Swept into the distance that
Splits tranquility from movement
A stutter in some rumination's arch

The three women behind me
Could've been anything African

Lenient

Rechargeable shudders
of alchemic impressions
dance you upstairs
to the bottle and the lights.
The stars in the trees,
reflecting like the light
in the windows
and the lights in the bottles
damage your already messed up vision.
You let the dance
caffeinate you loose
and pull at your own heartstrings,
expecting to see the masses
fading further into a storm
that passes
every so often like a bad guesser.
The only people who work carry boxes.
You carry tunes
in your head that are like empty boxes.

Flight From North Carolina Home

---unspools across retentions
however
seventy times seven equals four hundred and ninety
leaves falling like imitations of a woman I loved so much in a not
to be way that I wish so much was and had something to do with
the same story as before with only slightly different details
saved like other stories told from a place that exists because I
made it exist

fall in love
if no more than once
get to know yourself too
there's no pressure
as you are so beautiful
and seem dedicated to the poem that's written in your DNA

Everything's Love

Like after a storm
That unfolded open to augment

Like chords you stumble upon
As what you want comes down

And then rises gently
And beautifully and calmly

Before as though salvation
Were a simple and unique

On-going process that defies
Gravity

The apple falling onto Isaac Newton's
Grailed mind and perfectly jumbling

The singular way
A number unaccounted for

Makes up infinity
To provide love's understanding

That hollers in the wind's gust
Towards liberation-divine

Knuckleheads

Enduring closes
the hours before
the darkness
to the heart

like mandalas
found next
to black holes
and restricted

by crafted icons,
an inherited refrain
praising itself,
silence approaching leaves,

regenerating as karma.
Sing within as you've
been told to do.
Sing within

the confessing
freedom worships
like clouds watching
a baby bird fly

for the first time,
hatchling of the mind.
Sing within shapes

you've created. Sing
within the releasing
of your desire, betrayal
underneath the taken heat.

It seems the heat is
all there is sometimes

King's Blues

My queen done died
And left me all alone
I been cried and cried
Sitting here on my throne

I ain't got no child
And this castle feels like the wild

No, the jester can't cheer me up
No matter how much wine is in my cup

Judge Not

I miss my father
Have my whole life

The streets have
Their own consonance

How the sidewalks
Meet the driveways

And the roads trail
Into the sky's divulging

I miss my father
So much I cry

At times
And hope

My fate
Is my own

For Passion

Seeing the rock
With protests painted on

Smoothly
I went forward

On the path
As always

Home is hope
Under a tree

The temple raises
That which is

Nothing before
Wrought in purity

A spirit turns the speech
Into a testimony

Rejoicing in the belief
Like souls of the bestowers

I wait for the stream's movement
I marvel at the sunset's piercing

Open across the horizon
Splotching changes

As minutes examine seconds
Towards a night's sedation

Healing

a first love
improper in hypothesis
might puncture the sails
sinking the crew

but
I
then
cracked with desire
was salvaged inward
and racing away from darkness

Encounter With Anti-Gravitational Forces That Curate

I should've been *there*   there
Beside the circuiting preacher
I might not have spoken about
              Breaking free and the body and the cage and the
dance and The One I Love

Like all the rivers running into the sea
Who will commune with me

Protecting my heart
as though awakening
was all you need
eternity over the sun

I
Go
Up

Because the law evoked
me as I evoked the law
as a lost perception of self
The singer would develop
Her particular treasure
As her last weapon

On Royal Street   incarnating wisdom
          into divided empty

Yet

I am working right now
sorrow's conceit the last memory as thought remembering that
the field
is never grateful for the rain and the rain
dripping down the saxophones' phosphor and mother of pearls
        owes nothing
Misread in that sensitivity

Like how we all make mistakes
Planting time where there are no graves

Recognized as the preeminence holding the description
I see a pile of fried oysters and smell hush puppies

At a rowdy place that has the word
Daddy in it

Como Foam Party

They wanted some, advocated
by the 21st century. Loving not the world, you
blacked out in the foam, still dancing to pretty
lights, the mafia, church and transfers casting

upon you. You wanted out, unknown like
the appearance when it happens, purified.

But you had to stay. Here is love. The bad
teacher and the solicitor agreed and had
one good record but you knew they were
liars, frauds, and nothing much more.

I Am Letting It Go

Drawing the masterpiece as an electromagnetic investor,
The Artist extends nature.

Appreciate truth and lies.
Grow, spirit, from within as the truth ignores the lies,

Experience abundances
as a magnificent swing
of consciousness
in smokey hazes of oneness
learning from perseverance
about what was and is and is going to be.

It Is Done

A man with two moons in his eyes
Wearing clouds

Told me
Your time is now
And then he asked me
What time is it?

    So
I strode into yet another new
                        echo
Calling
Over Basie and Brubeck

In a way I can't remember the specifics of
Which is unfortunate

Because all that is wanted is for you to remember the brand
Come on in and get your beard trimmed
come on now
you know you need it

That which they worshipped
An image popping like a bullet from a civil war's gun
Whispered to the host about me
I had made it to the end
Blessed like the dead
Somewhere standing on a sea of glass

Staring at the sun
The fearful clown deciding not to care

Deciding to tell the audience everything that night
A lapse in time
And the battered woman
Who wrote about blind werewolves and vampires smelling love
In a different and made-up time
And who smiled only if something genuinely made her

Got drunk
Like she never learned how to drink

Like me
Like she taught herself how to drink at her childhood castle
Reaching for some Jack out of the top cabinet
Then putting water in to replace

Like me
She liked me
And my ghost stories
Which I can tell you if you want

Blessed as the watcher with layers on
I introduce The Hero to The Prophetess

Reciting Shakespeare
I looked to the east

Somewhere standing with a saxophone
Fela played
     And we played
With Fela

Rudiments on congas
That belonged to a stranger
I'd never meet
As we only meet those we are supposed to

The Head Chemist

Meditation to break manacles

Witnesses made unaware as we watched nine's animation

As I had been instructed

Leaving Hindsight

In the hills,
gratefully praying,

drifting, I am found,
compassion behind me.

If we all hold our hands up
together, Time won't matter.

I don't want to come down,
bitten and hungry and revived,

a stark light restating
the reservation as vision.

I should've yesterday.
As you do a ball, Time passes.

Gone into
multiplication,

we should've
repented earlier.